Squalls

Squalls

Poems by

Ed Ruzicka

© 2024 Ed Ruzicka. All rights reserved.
This material may not be reproduced in any form, published,
reprinted, recorded, performed, broadcast,
rewritten or redistributed without
the explicit permission of Ed Ruzicka.
All such actions are strictly prohibited by law.

Cover design by Shay Culligan
Cover photo taken by the author
on an island in the Mississippi River
Photo of the author taken by friend
Nancy-Von Brock at Spili, Crete

ISBN: 978-1-63980-507-5

Kelsay Books
502 South 1040 East, A-119
American Fork, Utah 84003
Kelsaybooks.com

To my constant one, Renee Stickels.

To my brothers and sisters of the word: Clare Imholtz, Gary Beaumier, Jane Napolitano, John Tarlton, Charles deGravelles, Carolyn Ricapito, Ben & Eileen Shieber, Andrew King, Jeanne George, Marilyn Shapley, Cynthia Toups, Randolph Thomas, Ray Berthelot, Michael Newell, Robert Wexelblatt, who have suffered me through this book and more.

. . . pitiful, beautiful human.
—Ellen Bass, "How to Apologize"

Remember that even the road to terrible battles
Always passes by gardens and windows
And children playing and a barking dog.
—Yehuda Amichi, "Huleikat, The Third Poem about Dickey"

Acknowledgments

Thank you to the following publications, in which versions of these poems previously appeared:

Call Me: "Black Dutch"
Canary: "What Survives"
Jerry Jazz Musician: "Missing Matt"
Mason Street Literary Journal: "Becky"
New Millennial Writing: "My Lungs Are a Shambles"
Open: Journal of Arts & Letters: "All That Then"
The Poet Magazine: "Bounty and Thanks"
The Poetry Buffet: An Anthology of New Orleans Poetry: "It Is Raining Again"
Porch Press: "Sunday Reading at the Maple Leaf" (Maple Leaf Rag Anthology VII)
Pure Slush Press: "Blown" (Wrong Way, Go Back Anthology), "The House Painter" (Love Anthology), "On Gary Publishing His Second Book" (Friends Anthology), "Greek Coffee" (Pride Anthology)
The Rat's Ass Review: "Naming Leaves"
The Red Eft Review: "How Fishing Went for Us"
Silver Birch Press: "Warblers, Ibis, Sparrows, Bittern, Kingfishers"
Snapdragon Journal of Art & Healing: "Redemption Song"
The Stickman Review: "Earnings"
Thema Magazine: "Danged If You Do"
Truth Serum Press: "What I Like" (Indigomania Anthology)
Verse Virtual: "On This Saturday in August," "My Heart Is a Shambles," "It Is Raining Again," "The House Painter," "The Dancers," "Folding Church Chair," "That Trigger of Release"

Contents

CHAPTER I Squalls and Mud Pies

Mississippi River Pies	17
On This Saturday in August	19
How Fishing Went for Us	20
My Heart Is a Shambles	22
The Going	23
Etude in E-minor	25
"The General" in the Rain	26
Tangerine	28
Redemption Song	29
Naming Leaves	30
What Survives	32
The Sweepers	33
Insinuations of Rain	34
Hurricane Harvey in Baton Rouge	35
What I Like	36
Swelter, a Weather Report	37
Flood	39
My Budget Summer Vacation	40
Blown	41
For Helen or Henry	42

CHAPTER II Faces

Carolyn	45
Becky	46
The House Painter	47
The Thirteenth Note	49
Missing Matt	53
O-m-m-e-g-a-n-g	55
That Trigger of Release	56

Jacks in the Deal	57
Who Purged Himself the Hard Way	58
By the Door	60
At Albertsons I Come to Understand	61
On Gary Publishing His Second Book	62

CHAPTER III Off the Grid

Pup	65
Earnings	66
Spring on My Patio	68
Warblers, Ibis, Sparrows, Bittern, Kingfishers	70
It Is Raining Again	72
Wasted Nights	73
Greek Coffee	74
The Dancers	75
Folding Church Chair	76
Summer Shivers	78
I'm a Magpie on Dauphine St.	80
Raw	82
My Drug of Choice	83
Danged If You Do	84
Sunday Reading at the Maple Leaf	85
Corner of Royal and Franklin, 8:20 AM	86

CHAPTER IV Meditations

There Wasn't Much of a Winter	89
I Talk to a Dove	90
Carolina	91
Out Late in the Atchafalaya Basin	92

West	93
I Cling to What I Can	94
At Big Bend National Park	95
January	96
Bounty and Thanks	97

CHAPTER V On Becoming

Yes, It Was an End	101
How to Heal	103
I Had Fallen	104
All That Then	105
I Gave It Up	106
Why I Don't Drink Tequila	107
Somehow, January 2017	109
The Obvious	110
Black Dutch	111
The Weight	112
Valentine	113
Dusk	114
Again	115
My Sixty-Fifth Spring	116

CHAPTER I

Squalls and Mud Pies

Mississippi River Pies

I gathered armloads of wood
to send up a bonfire on the head of an island
pointed north to cleave a river current
that spreads its sand wide as any city park.

Later I stopped, bent to knee
and pointed down then up so you would see
with eyes that swirled everywhere back then
a rippled moon in water's pitch, then the other moon on high
and a comet fell through the body of the night,
momentary jewels between the cleavage of cumulus.

But what comes back strongest is how the next day
in a state that loses its sky to earth whole seasons on end
in the topsy-turvy swell of these gullies, sloughs, bayous
and their ooze, I found you mid-morning
mud splotched and plopped into slop.

In your tiny swimsuit you slapped small palms against earth
worked the flour of that muck with a ludicrous, full-tilt bravado.
With your half-formed tongue, the type
not ready to tell much of anything
about this fury and trembling we go through
you worked that muscle at the back row
of itty-bitty tombstone teeth to turn
breath, syllables and body into song.

Beloved daughter, absolute angel formed
out of nothing but blind hope and blunder—
you sang out with a pride that was forming you already
"Daddy, I know the recipe for mud pies."

All morning long as I sat in shade and read
you slapped up mud pies, brought them to bake
on the log behind me. Baked more
after we got back home and on into October
my excellent one. You did that for nothing but love
scrumptious love and mastery of the world through love.

On This Saturday in August

Because thunder. Because branches
are being swept by wet wind. Because
house frames in Houston steam as mold forms
and a fifth of that city is in motels
or on relative's couches. Because
birds are being blown backwards.

Because aisles at Home Depots
are still overcrowded as we struggle to
recover from last year's hundred-year event.
Because the sun is about to be blocked by moon.

Because there is clamorous rage
every time any state statue of the looming dead
raised to reiterate tyranny gets filed away
into storerooms, is smothered under cloaks.

Because I went to the hospital to visit
a friend whose eyes have gone faint.
Breath irregular and labored.
Because I am back home to watch
two squirrels race along phone lines
where rats also trot in moonlight.

Because sun and moon are about to get
things all mucked up. Although her mouth
is always moist and open toward mine
there is suddenly too much space here
too much day seeking balance, so that

the city closes its eyelids in the rain
to sing a song drenched
in despair and awakening
in a voice of rich splendor.

How Fishing Went for Us

July showers sweep in on depot schedules, 12:47, 2:39.
Sink the city in sheets of gunmetal, putty, pewter.
Disperse summer's oven until air gets breathable again.
A sudden school of minnow gusts into the oaks
rattles those branches with ten thousand scales of cool, cool silver.

This is how it was for us when I used to walk you down the block
up one more. Then turn a wandering left until we came under
that stand of spruce you thought was a forest, creaky
and frightful—ripe for the wolf's paw or the witch's cowl.

Except that we were just across from a white, dilapidated house
where Nicolette and I once went peddling Girl Scout cookies
and got invited into an oil-cloth kitchen by a woman who tottered
above her cane. One who couldn't spare a dollar or her tabby
would go fishless for days. So we returned weeks later
with boxes of Thin Mints and told her they were excellent
kept in the freezer and even better crumbled over vanilla ice cream.

She said, "But I don't have anything to give you." Then
made us weak tea we couldn't get away from fast enough
as she spent the whole time scuttling around
scraping together a tote-bag of marbles
one time-hardened Tootsie Roll, photo
of her middle boy by the Sunday shore in San Diego
and the fuzzy torsos of yellowjackets cased in amber.
She forced the bag into my hand as we sailed off
hailing our "So longs" forever and anon.

On an afternoon like this under tall pine I might completely
undo one of my shoelaces to lay across your tiny palm.
You would cast it out upon the waters of the puddle
that always formed at that low spot. I remember those days
tasting like aluminum as I stood, my mind overcome by sky
as any puddle can become while a daughter sings softly
so that fish will drift in. Your song a sort of lure
as every song is, that caught us nothing those days but now
seems to be catching everything, here, I could ever want.

My Heart Is a Shambles

The woman I love loves cats.
She strokes them. The mirror
is a harsh, empty winter.

In high school I was hog tied
held down, branded, set loose.
I solved that by molting.

It's a tease really—talents given
what is expected from these ongoing
engines of desire. Reminds me

of how I reeled after deep
tongue kisses outside the dorm
with college girls when they knew
they weren't going all the way.

Vast tides of fire rose from my thighs.
Then a flood of expectations. A wife
who woke at four to be alone. Was alone.
Gave us two infants that thrived, left.
I left. The children left.

I had something I lost. I want
something others have. Tomorrow
is around one more hard corner.

This morning having gone out
my back door after coffee, I have
before me, under the mammoth
teat of a milky aurora and after

last night when the stars fell
down by the millions, now, while
creeks crackle and hiss, I have this,
one wheelbarrow full of rain.

The Going

        I

The wind is restless, searching.
Wind reaches into rooms, pulls
readers' eyes out toward sky.
"What is headed my way?" eyes ask.

Wind burrows into the chests of trees
shakes limbs as if whole forests
have been asleep for millennia
and it is time for them
to pull sodden roots out of earth.
Time again to march forward
giants whose steps shake fields
send monstrous shadows before them
across the openings of dens where
badger, wolf and rabbit curl
embryonic, in a womb of earth.

Our city radiates from a bend in a river
that tries every spring to overflow
and fill city streets with catfish, eel
swirling hordes of river shrimp.
Still, the city has enough muscle
to keep the river moving alongside it
a mere song in the throat of the land.

        II

When I walk into the wind
it seems I am peeling and also
rising up from the streets
of our city its docks, hospitals, hunger.

Suddenly I have no voice of my own.
I have to borrow the sounds of house timbers
groaning whines through pine needles
frantic rhythms as branches beat the nearest branch.

Tree limbs lift up to become the arms of praise
without any object of praise.
I blow into the chests of living things.
I fill them and go on. I go on.

Etude in E-minor

Under this monolithic sky
leaves and grass can't even
get enough light to glisten.
Rain drifts down light
as mosquitos' feet.

I work alone in a room
I built to work alone, room
detached from the house.

Yesterday hospice
came into the home
of my sister. Gave her
a hospital bed that folds.
A mattress accomplished
in cradling the dying.

I braid syllables, strike
fire to words, sketch
the slender curves of birds' throats
wrestle with the agitation
of the sea and agitation
in the bowels of men.

I tap, strike, fix
an inconsolable
sequence of letters
in the key of e-minor

and stay hounded by what
I cannot get right.

"The General" in the Rain

Today I see a man whose nerves quietly fire
under white sheets. Tic by tic nerves jolt
his flesh toward firm as stone. He cannot sit up.
Cannot turn over without help. This man
is in a state of transformation, is becoming
a sculpture of himself draped in a sheet.
The man's eyes have to do his talking
call upon the entire reach of their vocabulary
to say what they can of patience and grief.

Earlier I drove through rain, saw it part then surge.
When it rains, the emergency room loads up
from car wrecks, but they are often the lucky ones.
A fracture, a cast, crutches, then they go on.
There are so many floors at the General.

In another room a woman has lost her vision
for everything but her son and her husband.
They visit, sit hour upon hour. She has lost
her eyes for trees, for clouds. Lost her eyes
for the pouring, the splashing out of water.
For the quiet slant-shaded corners of rooms
where others move through her sorrow.

Months pass slowly in this labyrinth of grief
and recovery. Storms are common.
A sea hangs itself above the city to slowly
incrementally descend onto roofs, streets, gutters.
Mothers can't cure their babies' colic, hearts seize
and then I read that our legislature has finagled
a way to squeeze even more out of the working poor
gift it to those in gated communities.

I was in room 644 with a woman whose hands trembled
so terribly that she dropped a tissue. Then she couldn't hold
one of those flimsy plastic cups half-full of water.
Her hand trembled with the rapid staccato rhythm
of a young rabbit's heart after I plucked it up
and held it to my chest decades ago near a creek. The rabbit
wanted badly to break free the way we all do, especially
when we graduate from high school. Except not many do.
We stay locked within grief and have too few words for it.

Tangerine

After a frayed day
loose ends, exhaustion
rain sifts straight-lined, windless
but also cut by sunset shafts
that angle in through
pine, sycamore and oak.

Grass slathered slick.
Thirst of landscape. Bamboo
shimmers in glissando.

At the end of a day or decade
a man wants done something
his hands did. Alone, bone-hollow

I stand in drizzle's whispers, vespers
with only what falls to the tongue.
Sibilance and syllable.

Sifts of rain but enough
that run-off wriggles
sinks into muck.

My skin is silvered, wet.
At arm-hair's tips
hints of tangerine.

Redemption Song

for Charles deGravelles

The homeless sleep on concrete under the bridge.
Look up seventy feet to see the musculature
of the river reflected as it weaves on steel beams.

Light cannot touch them in their shadows
except when moon sizzles across waves
dazzles into eyes and lays its web upon
the flat slabs of the bridge's buttresses.

Songs the homeless know: rain's tempos
dawn in a bird's throat, fluting and arches
of possum bones, what the young bring down
in restless circles as they trade jibes
or go off in pairs to squelch gasps
under bushes near the river's lapping.

Against big odds, homeless sleep
with the roar of bullish trucks above.
Sleep to the gnash of gear on gear.
A corridor of air furiously ripped open.
Tires' whine, the baffle of exhaust.
It takes a lot to sleep. It's harder now
to get the cocktail of booze and meds to right.

Once you drift, you might get lifted back
to the place where you grew up
along the banks of this river.
Cane fields ran and flowed forever.
Ribbons, off stalks rattled, drenched in wind.
Blackbird and crow landed, clung.
Dark feathers splayed in strong wind.

Naming Leaves

Six days after the great ice storm
so chilling that it knocked fear of Covid
straight out of our brains
I hold baby Henry in my arms.

We are in my daughter's backyard
and already engulfed in a soft
spring turn of sky. An owl
calls from inside a magnolia.

Baby Henry looks at a bush
its leaves shriveled by recent ice.
He raises an arm, points a finger.
Says "Phooof." Shifts the finger
two inches, says "Vvuuu."

Now Henry turns his attention
to the wings of a fern.
He can't yet fully extend
that index finger. It curls
in the direction of a frond.

Eyes luminous as twin moons
Henry focuses on a single leaf, says
"Tthaaa." Again, even softer, "Whough."

In the aftermath of the storm's destruction
Baby Henry has purposed himself
to naming, one by one, the leaves
and then, I guess, each grass blade
every stitch of rain that falls
downward through his gaze

so that I might come to know them
as he does and to understand
how to turn any afternoon
into a slow benediction.

What Survives

The six creeks that drain this city are periodically
cleared to ensure that heavy rains get swept away.

Laborers yank apart jammed branches where turtles perch
and plastic bags snare. Workers haul out tires, planks

break up dams from which moccasin and blue runners hunt.
Minnows dart around rubber boots. Before their advance

kingfishers and egret reposition themselves along the bank.
Rusted culverts, dryers, golden rod, vines, bamboo.

A few blocks from our house the creek runs green-grey
except at night when water segues to black.

Under moon: coyote, skunk, raccoon. They leave
paths trampled through thorn and scrub but a man

needs a machete or at least a strong stick to force
his way through bramble along mucked bank.

At points, creek slopes have been reinforced by a scrabble
of shattered pavement, massive, silt-settled slabs.

Less and less any wandering boys. Less and less the squeals
of children. Hub caps, homeless men, things dislodged.

Behind Broadmoor Junior High, just above where a tributary
crashes in, is a dandelion knoll sequestered enough for teens

to smoke cigarettes and to offer their virginity up to an imperfect
wilderness. Owls, lichen. Stars upside down in the pitch of night.

The Sweepers

It is finally fall in Louisiana. I sweep patio leaves
on Armistice Day, thinking of fallen soldiers
debris and fragility. I can imagine Lee Harvey
Oswald sweeping leaves in Metairie, Louisiana.

But not Ruby or Calley, Sirhan or Manson sweeping
or really any of the murdering terrorists that came
behind the assassins. None of them lived in homes.
They lived in apartments, makeshift places.

Except those so misfit they still lodged in
their parents' backrooms or basements plotting
things parents can't ever imagine of their children.
But none would sweep leaves the way parents do

for decades, through seasons before and after
their children go off as soldiers or marry
policemen or give birth to doctors that
can't save every soldier that curses and

plays cards and pays hookers before they
finally fall and get carried out of the belly
of a military transport aircraft at dead midnight
or in the brilliance of morning light bounding

off a concrete runway. Get carried out in caskets
by other soldiers with wills as firm as theirs.
While I sweep, the sky is blue as a robin's egg
and seems that fragile, the same way infants

are fragile in their parents' arms. Are heavy
and light at once as we all go on sweeping
and making babies because hope blinds us
lifts, twirls us, hope floats us, light as leaves.

Insinuations of Rain

This front roils like a child
let loose at the fair, a child
that dashes off, lurches
shoots and wheels.

Wind muscles in.
Branches swoop
this way, that
in a symphony
of absolute becoming.

Chimes suspended from branches
toll like bells on a ferry boat
that nods through thick fog.

Flower petals lift to sample
trace minerals in the air.
Arabesques of wind.

Even the hairs on my arms rise
as this city breathes like a lover
who has thrown aside the sheets.

Hurricane Harvey in Baton Rouge

It is raining. Rain is in the forecast.
Rain is in the ditches. Kingdoms
of rain, tall turrets, moats.

Monday, Tuesday, Wednesday
all of them expect to be
swallowed in a great gargling
throat of rain. Gutters, gullies bubble
with a constant swish and toll.

A hurricane seeks warm water
hungers, feeds, throws down cold.
Seeks a shape, convection, funnel, order
and wracks the coast with chaos.

Cool, unflinching tumbles of silver here.
Drips, splats, shiny as stainless
Thanksgiving knifes, a carving-
up-the-landscape-rain.

The thin and the thick of it
on us in dark and leaving
less of light each day.
There was a sun. The moon tried
to blot it. Rain is doing that one better.

Nearby, in Houston, rivers puff up
above their banks, thread through
swing-set metal, gush down streets.
How do these trees still shimmer their hundred
shades of emerald, thousand shades of jade?

What I Like

That instant when nerves fire
flare to muscle shovel blade
out from muck's suction

and all comes up mad with facets flashing.
Rain's slivers, crumpled foil, lead
shine in the shovelful.
Fast streams, wet mounds, beads.

Sludge fades back to black
and dun by the time
I get it slopped out
sloping down a pile.

Two quick ticks only
before earth's pailful of blue
regathers down in the hole.
Shoots up intense.
That fire of azure reflects
restful. Back to what it was
walled by clay.

Nearby a dove sends its cool
grotto of a coo out. So I rest
elbow atop the shovel
for a few spasms
of a gurgling heart.

The coolness of wet dirt
on palm and fingers
as I massage bush roots in.
Muscle work. Just that
and that and that.

Swelter, a Weather Report

Bones soft as soup bones
awash where dun bayous
slither, slosh through muck.
Days on end great rivers
sun themselves, laze dull-eyed
as glutted snakes that stay
too full, too enraptured
to budge one murky inch.

Our waters loll, soft and lush
with swishes of sines inside soil
that yields silt rinsed in rainfall.
In daylight we get a suspension
of droplets that loose their flow
through the green ventricles of leviathan oak.
Droplets feed fern, moss, mold, lichen
fungus, mushroom over the striations
of live oak's long and muscled limbs.

Air so rich we can almost sip it,
tipple our sunsets. A jasmine tea
sets its cup of dawn onto patio furniture.
Birds stroke, swim under
ponderous pewter cloud banks.
Noon brings its thousand
blades of kitchen knives. Steel light
rasps its edge across our hides.

I would leave this room. I would go
to the banks, dart naked as a minnow
nose through twines of current.
Dip into the delight of cold caverns
every river carves into its map.
I would put myself where bars
look bent in what bends light.

I would sally off. I say, "Sally off,"
but for the multitudinous silk
webs spiders have spun over
the sparrow bones of these feet.
I can only flinch in this
great furnace of light.

Flood

for Big Junior and Tricia Freeman

Immobilized in driveways, car roofs formed
a temporary archipelago all along
Durnin Drive as Wildlife and Fishery boats
sent wakes against doors and windows.

Kittens clung to tree branches. A moccasin
sunned on a mailbox. In the house I found
three guitars had boated all over the living room
water still in their boxes. Sealed
tight as a casket, the fridge had
tipped and rolled, settled on its side over the sink.

Rugs sodden. Plaster and frame-wood swollen
in heat like the walls had a case of bursitis.
Fungal, deadly but I'd had to go
to get back in before the adjusters
made false ledgers of what we'd lost.

All any guitar here can play anymore is
this flood, what remains, what was swept away.
I have a single Gibson I salvaged to slide
fingers over strings, frets. Bend notes.

Tricia and I sit just out the door of room 126
at a La Quinta thirty miles up the interstate.
Quick picks, streams, ribbons of notes float
out into the tire whine and trailer rattle
from I-10 as streetlamp light settles
and pools on parking lot asphalt.

My Budget Summer Vacation

Wanna say whiskers of rain. Wanna say
long broom straws of rain come in
sweeping what were clouds of dust
that billowed up from farmer's tractor tires
to coat weeds and wildflowers all along our roadsides.
Sweep bitty-bit, dried-up ladybug pee
and the wee pooh of beady-black ants.

None of it stands still, swept by this rain
of broom straws down to gully-gush
gutter whoosh, till the panorama
shoots glitter-bright when sun rips
the curtain of clouds back open.

Wanna say whiskers, oh whiskers
oh whiskers of rain came in close to grampa-kiss
this whole day into bloom again.
Bounce me on your knee, grampa-day. Balloon me
big sky, bright-n-light all the while away.

I like how wind makes the hammock swoop.
The hammock's as hard to get out of as a dream.
So I stay under leaves so plentiful
it'd take any computer some sorta very long
to calculate all the amount of green crinkling above
like a currency of ecstasy in oak, magnolia, myrtle.

That's where the wind loves to spend its time
while whiskers of rain come all over my
can't-get-out-of-the-hammock
summer afternoon that just clicks
blue again. Balloons. Whisks
me up and dreams me down
till I'm gone. Gone, gone. Gone.

Blown

for Michael Newell

Christ sakes, the way this
wind saws up in oaks.
Shingle-tearer. Suit-tail-whipper
straight out of the southeast.

Hauling half the gulf up.
Dumping it on the city.
Drenching cats in alleys.
Too much wind to think straight.

Cars wreck at corners. Sirens.
E. R. nurses scamper and squawk
while doctors write out scripts
wrists working quick as a drummer's.

Only the old women able to
stay their places streetside, stable
as bookends. Get in and out the
Dollar Store without any fuss.

Barbers sit in empty seats. Gaze
at eighteen-wheelers that haul by
like whales. I made it home.
Poured myself a stiff one.

Found a work glove on the patio
blown down off a table, drenched
sopping and flat. Sad that, but no sadder than
the toddler that wailed in the back of the bus
all the way from downtown.

For Helen or Henry

January under a tender rain.
Beads dangle at the tips
off slender crepe myrtle branches.

I see these often enough
as I go to get my morning paper
four hundred transitory jewels.

Each holds a reflection of the world
as valid as any I will get from the day's news
but they usually go unnoticed.

Today I pause to see these diamonds hang
as rounded as my youngest daughter's belly
as she carries her firstborn toward its dawn.

CHAPTER II

Faces

Carolyn

who is nine hundred miles from our arms
as her husband takes her temperature every hour
whose skin has turned to a frail parchment
starlight tattoos with its needles
whose ribs ached all night as an owl
forced the moon in and out of its chest

who comes to our patio every summer
to flash blue eyes her mother gave her
eyes we do not want diminished to mere mirrors

who annually paints the shoreline of Maine and Georgia
because she knows what it is to be fiercely alone
and is right now alone in the way she has always known
on a shore never advertised in travel magazines

who drank sunlight from over our own Mississippi River
as it made its way to be drowned and reborn
and drowned in the Gulf of Mexico
and then painted the river in oils on a canvas

who also painted the white flower in a wine bottle
I pulled out of the garbage on Rittiner Street
when I went to visit one day after
she had tried to purge herself of delusions
the way young people will do when they ignite
desperate to burn away any trace of their history

who is with us every summer on our patio
while sun throws burning lances down
and who I need here again with her bottled water
and laugh that barely escapes swallowing itself

who needs to be here again if I am
going to be able to go forward into
the landscape of all that is taken

Becky

In the ICU by the bedside where the respirator
breathed, I stood as if I were standing with you
on a cusp or a horizon in a slim bend of light
at an intemperate, almost foreign border.

You were silent as you had been for days, unable
to be anything other than silent, listless, discolored.
It was Thursday afternoon when I finally said
it would be all right if you wanted to stop.

Said that your daughter was driving up
from New Orleans. Would be where I was
soon—beside the bed—beside you along with Stuart.
That Stu was home at that very moment, tucking
sheets, tidying up a room of grief for your daughter.

You are behind the camera in all the crimson suffused
sunset photos of Florida beaches, the snapped shots
of the rest of us on Christmas Eve, the small bands
ringing the table you'd set, lifting glasses toward your lens.

There will never be another spoonful of turtle soup
without you there and not there. You've been
with me for every such sip at various and sundry
restaurants throughout south Louisiana since you made
that soup for the four of us one night in maybe '92.

Soup beside which all the rest have paled.
Though they have all been good enough, I guess
to keep me going through these days of tragedy
and joy where you will never be again. But still

a spoonful of soup, evening fog in oaks
certain lights in through window onto bric-a-brac
or under chair legs on a rug seize our hearts
and bring you back to us.

The House Painter

Though he was run off from Montrose High
as incorrigible, everyone asks for Dex because
"That man could paint a pinstripe on a rooster tail."
Dex keeps his lines impeccable, pays attention
to the most minute of details. "Never a reason to rush,"
he'll say while he exhales a Chesterfield.

Dex takes only high dollar calls.
One week he stirs a vibrant ochre
as a dentist's wife heads out for yoga class.
The next, he rolls jade up and down a hallway
while a politician in a back study
explodes a string of curses into a cell phone.
Dex parties and batches it until he turns 42.
Then he falls for a plump little number from Indiana
who is down here as a Century 21 regional manager.
They marry quiet-like at a Holiday Inn on Highway 17.

His wife gives Dex a ready-made family
as his of-a-sudden daughter turns eleven.
Dex takes to being a dad like a lab takes to pond water.
He is the one that carts the girl to soccer practice.
The girl blooms under the tutelage of Dex's level voice.
So Dex is sore oppressed two years in
when friends start to warn him about things
they see his wife posting on Facebook
which habit he has never quite established.

Seems the ambitious little lady from Indiana
is living large having hooked up
with a high roller in a crimson 'Stang
who is developing a subdivision
where there used to be a marsh.

Dex flat loves that woman and that little girl
better than he loves his Coors, though
his Coors proves to be the more reliable.

The Thirteenth Note

for Matt Lanius

                I

Scary thin, you puffed a home-roll
                In the halls of memory
just out the break door
                Its rabbit holes
Foot propped on a mop bucket.
                Its labyrinths

Your beautiful wife at a table with the other wives
                Subterranean.
One eye on a fire escape
                Time wrenched
The other toward the street.
                Memory

Exhausted—hands still alive with the raucous
                These were stories
celebration of a jam you'd just banged out.
                From before I knew you
Hands ready for another rip into drive, into fury.
                Things I was told.
Poised for a foray into purity. That elegant math
                Almost as alive as things I know
hard won, which was your primary path into being.
                Now down a corridor of oblivion.

II

First, there was everything before. Vietnam. The P. T. S. D.
Estrangements. By the time we met you had settled in
to a wary codger's series of dodges, haranguers, rectitude.
You played gigs at clubs, bars, bookstores. But sooner or later
some night you just wouldn't show up. You'd leave the rest
of the band there to curse. To fake its way through. You were
somewhere undone, grumbling at the night. Maybe the engine
didn't turn over, maybe your alarm failed to ring at 8 PM.
Your brilliant, brilliant, tender, steely, brilliant hands
fingering a cigarette in a mix of street and starlight.

III

Then fire tried to wipe you out, left you
mid-street, standing with a bike at your hip, two cats
three music books and *Thus Spake Zarathustra.*
Shivering, draped in a blanket. Having woken from
an afternoon nap to flames and curling smoke.

The fire started from overloaded circuits, crossed wires to
a computer, hot plate, lamps, two Kawai, a Roland keyboard.
You stood on Oxford Ave. across from the graveyard
where city founders' tombstones survive like broken teeth.
Watched as fire hoses drenched it all, as water dripped off char.
Stood with cats, a bike, four books. Which is most
of what you'd seemed to have in the first place.
To start again from scratch at 63 with nothing
more than those brilliant, steely, brilliant hands.

IV

Your last place was a sort of midget deed grant. A postage
stamp yard at the side of a cousin's city estate. A property
in probate adjacent to a nationally registered plantation
where busloads of Yankees came to learn what local herbs
slave women cut and diced into historic gumbos. All
stuff you loathed so well. Stuff you ranted against.

Nicholson Drive traffic intermittent as runway traffic with
its drag of tin ripping air, scored tires whining on asphalt.
The oak by your door a green dome of silence as I waited
to be let in. You were so slow to let anyone in anymore.
Finally, you'd turn the bolt. Let me edge past stacked lumber
down a narrow hallway to the unmade bed. To stacks
jumbles of books. One chair. Cigarettes snuffed in tins.

The apartment cramped as a Bolshevik's quarters
with its impossibly tiny kitchenette where you
juiced, where you brewed up java in a converted
closet too small to even fit a fridge. Hard corners, elbows.

All this offset by the miracles of time your
fingers conjured as cats glided under furniture
leaped, curled, stretched in arrow pose. Accomplished
yogis, bellies exposed, blissed-out while you
served up their daily doses of Beethoven.

V

Two pianos there. Two. One not enough. Your hands
needed more keys than they could ever get to. You said
"I finally learned how to play Mingus." Betsy told me.
"Do him like you're half drunk. Lean notes out, let them hang."

You played "Peggy's Blue Sky Light" the way Mingus
first meant it. Brought talcum shafts of distilled light in.
Had them sift across hours. Fall on this. Touch that.
Finally beams found tossed sheets, two lovers.

Then you gave something different. Something you
owned in your hands. Only you. Always. A keening
of light across distances. The architecture of constellations
small bells of the keys vibrated above a damper petal.
Light softly born or softly dying. The 13th note lain in its
bed of chords. Arcturus there, pristine and bright, set.

Missing Matt

In the end, they put his few pieces of handmade furniture
by the side of the street. One was the piano stand
crafted from skid-wood to perfectly match his height.

Sometimes he'd cross his legs, sit sidesaddle
dangle a hand-rolled cigarette off the edge of his lips
as I drank tea. He'd indulge me with Mingus.
Lift notes up from smolder, through dust motes
      into sapphire.

His cats had stopped sniffing him or had started
an agitated routine of sniffing him more.
Who's to say? The cats had stopped
hearing him balance exquisite delicacy
against cascades of illumination as Matt stroked out
a Beethoven Sonata with the same hands
that did not stroke their fur anymore.
Matt's brother let himself in with the hidden key
found Matt there. Cats don't weep.
      Brothers weep.

So much time is spent in every life
doing and undoing. Heat soup.
Slop and wash that pot. Slip beneath
sleep, re-straighten sheets. Swing open
walk through, close the door.

Except for a man like Matt
whose determination was devoted fervor.
Each pitch, its intensity, duration
was a choice he made, a step
into a definite way of being.

He fired off notes with such
unfailing commitment to tone
that phrases hung in the air
long after   his fingers
stopped,   sometimes
                     for years.

O-m-m-e-g-a-n-g

My ex's new husband Drew
spells letter by letter the name
of a favorite hand-crafted Lambic Wheat
or IPA evidently only his fine palate
could discover. Spells slowly
professorially. Always spits
on the hard Ps. Spells
letter by freakin' letter.
I think, "Thanks, bub
for all that sharing."

Later I come to surmise
that maybe after he's done
with his legions of notations, quotations
all the grading, after he has diapered
and tucked his octogenarian father
into a bed of fiery nightmares
Drew sits on his porch.

Shrubbery, shadows. Possum
make their way from nearby
drainage canals. Starlight elbows
through cloud cover. As an
intolerable heat releases
into tolerable darkness, Drew
eases beer down his throat
a release so potent, he is
compelled to spell it out.

That Trigger of Release

Mason came, still looking dangerous
as one of King Lear's besotted knights
still lurching right each step, hip hitched
by what must be stabbing lumbar pain.

You could hang a hammock, catch a nap
inside his slow Tennessee drawl.
Renee poured iced tea on the patio
while I finished in the garden.
Shoved bamboo shafts into
shoveled dirt. Looped twine.
Tied up tomato stalks.

When I finally settled into a chair
Mason was telling how a friend
called on a Saturday eight years ago
to say, "Turn on channel 141 now.
It's *Cops*." He saw his daughter there.
On a shadowed sidewalk, his daughter
propped up a tattooed lad whose ass
Memphis fuzz finally cuffed and hauled off.

He saw his own daughter on grimy
historic pavement. Beale Street, 3 AM.
She was fifteen. Sixteen when
Mason saw her on the tube; 24
now, doing sets and lights for some
struggling and amoebic theater troop.

It was good, so good to sit
and hear another's troubled pauses
as a thrush ducked into wisteria
with a flag-leaf in its beak. Good
to sit still and let the world reel.
Good to slide beer down my throat
as if I had no care.

Jacks in the Deal

My first brother-in-law, a company man, mostly scowled.
Glared even when family gathered. Was, at least
attentive to his mother as she grew older, frail, tottering.
First on cane, then slowly in procession with a walker.
Because he was the oldest, the family tended to meet
at his house, endure endless rounds of Nashville twang.
He'd tell us "Country is a white man's blues," as if he
were somehow downtrodden instead of just easy to ruffle.

Had another bro-in-law, later, different scenario
snapped into a sports coat, shirt open-collared
above layers of blubber. A man inwardly warm as a seal.
Unctuous. He'd grin, pump hands, everybody's in the room.
He hauled in bags of presents for the kids: stuffed unicorns
coloring books, gadgets—items plucked from airport stores.
He spent weekends on the cell checking contacts or crunching
numbers on his laptop with a bedroom door ajar. Would
blow a week's check to video-poker during lay-overs at O'Hare
Kennedy, Dulles. Had to hit his doctor-brother up for loans.

Been through enough marriages and hook-ups
to write a few of my own country classics by now.
Baggage. Have a new set of hard legs across
the holiday table these days. After dinner we
settle on the couch. Loosen belts. Watch helmets
crash into pads. Watch men wrestle each other to the dirt.
Lou gets up, asks, "Anyone, 'sides me, need a lil brewski?"

Who Purged Himself the Hard Way

for Barry Callihan

I said to myself, "Barry, I have to let you go
though I don't know where you have gone.
Though I now understand that I have never known
where you went when you went home."

It has been a long time since I felt
the air taken out of my lungs.
Felt like I must be underwater.
I know it has not been long for you.
You came under a large shadow
that could not be escaped
that cast itself over your days.

Soon, maybe even now, you are to be burned
by someone whose job includes the burning
of remains. Someone who will turn away
maybe take a swig of Coke, as a thick
rope of smoke rises out of you.

For the first time in years, you will
grow light. Light enough for your mother
to carry you in her arms again. Take you
to a place she knows you loved. A place
that stands empty most of the time.

What is left of your largess will be
sprinkled into wind, pepper grass.
Then rain. Rain and ash. Runs, quick
silvered ribbons, rushes. Creeks
surge into rivers that absorb surges
within their quiet banks, reflect the sky.

So I am letting you go, Barry
into dirt, into sky, into sea.
Letting you go with these words
that reach for the still place
the silent field. Quiet, now. Quiet.

By the Door

in memory of Fred DiGiulio

There will be others
tying off loops, colorful sprays
with clever knots to make
a lure true enough to get
a bass to strike because a bass
sees with its Paleolithic eye
the image of an insect that
bass have feasted on for eons.
But Fred is gone.

There will be others
to walk the dry cordilleras
of the Rockies' Mexican spine
where butterflies
winter in droves
but Fred is gone.

There will be others
to cook for family and friends
that perfect jambalaya
buttered oysters on the grill
but Fred is gone.

And the one who comes
in dreams is slender
as a shadow—the way
light bends around
a figure by the door
where Fred has gone.

At Albertsons I Come to Understand

The cashier tells me she has two jobs.
She goes to the second without
seeing her kids. She has three children.
Her mother helps them with homework.
Neither can help with the math.
Her oldest son is starting to back talk.

The cashier's mother says they all live
with her because she owns the house.
The cashier tells people that her mother
lives with her. The cashier pays the bills
all the bills. Her mother's meds run high.

Her middle child made the Youth Orchestra
last October—oboe. There are three
concrete steps with no rail by the street
and four more to the porch. After she
gets off the kids are already down
for the night. Streetlamps diminish
the stars. Some nights it takes
time to make it up those steps.

On Gary Publishing His Second Book

for Gary Beaumier

Wave-glint narrows your eyes
as you walk your shoreline
consume the barren acts
of rock, breaker, dawn.

A seagull lifts, tilts as you step
over stone, ice, flotsam. Then inch
across a creek, frozen, arrested in motion
still hungry for April when the creek
can let its torrent find a final rest
in that great lake which you revere.

You have stayed alert, an adept
attuned to what morning coughs up.
The way a river grows straighter
swifter, cuts deeper through earth
our friendship has aged.

I live at the bottom end of the Mississippi's
voluptuous river basin where land
is protected by levees as the river's
accumulation of runoff and dreams—
whatever night has shed in Ohio,
Colorado, Minnesota, West Virginia—
surges. Sky reflects below my feet
as the current pulses between cow fields.

For the sake of this old river
for myself and for you, I ask
"How is it that after all these winters
fresh tributaries still spill into us?"

CHAPTER III

Off the Grid

Pup

My daughter, Miriam, and my wife
came upon a blind dog at a public pool
that kept wandering into the drink.
Big hearted, they fished him out
ferried him home swaddled in a towel.

Oddly, named the old fellow "Pup." Pup
became for me, a sort of matted rug that ate
shat and shuffled around for nine months.
When Pup died, I dug a hole in the back yard.

In the mornings pouring coffee
wife in the bedroom zipping her skirt
I'd spy Miriam alone out in the yard
gathering twigs, dandelions, violets.

She wandered on half-formed legs.
Brought death tiny, inadequate tributes
and sang in a voice so high and soft
that to this day I haven't fully recovered.

Slowly as dawn evaporated dew
from grass blades, she began to learn how
there is nothing anyone can do but sing.

Earnings

You might as well count raindrops
in an August storm as try to calculate
how many nails I've pursed between lips
so I wouldn't have to reach back down
as I hammered, roofed, framed.

I remember soaking in grey as I sat
in the half-light of a factory break
to munch a cheese sandwich
beside a machinist that washed
his Twinkie down with Coke.
That was in Wisconsin.

In Louisiana, on a drilling floor, I threw a chain
that choked and twisted the diamond-head bit
off the end of one-hundred-twenty stands
of six-inch pipe stacked in ninety-foot sections
in the derrick-hand's rack, heavy wood floor
smeared with oil, black and slick.

I've helped lift a three hundred-fifty-pound woman
and then taught her how to use her muscle's pulleys
to leverage, to heft herself up from the bed onto a walker.
Then inch heavy feet across the floor
so she could live alone again.

Until you have a child you don't know
what you will do for a child. Or what
your parents did. How they worked beyond
tolerance until strain degraded their bones.
How they became consumed by a weariness
they had to pull themselves out of before dawn.
Hope that the future could cure them.

What can you do? Maybe, like mom
put it in a picture album so some day
you'll know, this was all worth saving.

Read the story that puts your toddlers to sleep.
Listen intently to what Rachmaninoff does
with piano keys. On the swing-set at the park
push those munchkins as high as their glee can manage.
Daily run a few miles along a slender stream.
Suit up for the graduations. Change engine oil
every thirty-five-hundred miles.

Finally, finally, finally let dusk find you
at the end of a glass mixing shadow and light.
Lift another sacred evening to your thankful lips.

Spring on My Patio

Gulf winds toss our Mexican petunias
wag and whoosh the lustrous riots of branches
that erupt in great, fluid swaths around us.
Mushroom clouds of vegetation explode
in every direction twelve months a year here
where oaks even sprout and root in roof gutters.

Yesterday afternoon I, a man who curses freely
and has not believed in prayer for decades
stopped on the stairs, crossed myself twice
out of deeply ingrained habit, fell silent.

I had just tried to stand a woman
in room 422 but stopped short after
blood began to seep from the staples
of a wicked incision that dove from sternum
to the basket of her pelvis. With supple hands
and a warm cloth, her nurse cleaned her.

It's been this way for a month. A surgeon
washes the wound out. Some new infection breeds.
She languishes. One line drips antibiotics through
a needle plunged into a chasm of the heart.
Another in the crook of her elbow flushes her
full of morphine, moonlight, abeyance.

One of her daughters sits in the room
reads, no doubt, prays and curses.
None of it does any good, except that prayer
brings us somewhere worth being, and curses
multiply the energy we need in any given moment.

This morning at least half of me is still
back in that room of yesterday. Nothing else
stops, waits for us or for prayer to catch up.
Not these winds, not the infinitesimal generation of cells
in the nourishing dark of intestinal folds.

But I am also here on my patio
where Mexican petunias raise purple trumpets
blast forth, flourish without any intention
of stopping, look best in spring wind.

Warblers, Ibis, Sparrows, Bittern, Kingfishers

Even swaddled, Baby Henry wriggles
as if a worm works inside him.
He spits up onto cotton draped
over my daughter's shoulder.
I call Baby Henry "Killer" because
my daughter is one of the new-minted
Fatimas whose eyes flash above masks
as she whisks into patient's rooms
attends them bedside, orders new meds.

Martin, her husband, is even more at risk
in the ICU where he has to force
feeding tubes down sedated throats
as a machine fills failed lungs. Both carry
the hospital home to wee bean Henry.
Neither lets us within ten feet of our little pip.
No telling what might have found its way
into the frail birdcage of his ribs.

Renee and I stand on the lawn.
The three of them stay by the door.
Martin shows us what they call "Superman."
Martin puts Baby Henry tummy down
over his shoulder. Sleepy Henry stretches
halfway straight, maybe too dangerously close
to an unseen load of Kryptonite.

The next weekend we take the canoe out.
Oars on knees, wind nudges us under
cypress branches luminous as lettuce.
A yellow-bibbed bird lights, fluffs
six feet above Renee's shoulder. Maybe
a vireo, maybe a warbler? Let's go with vireo.

Back out in the lake we drift through dozens
of birdcalls, each an illegible signature
with its own set of runs, quavers, fades.

I barely know a handful. Maybe I'll
recognize more by the time I get young Henry
into a boat, row him around, teach him to keen
into the silence behind all the birdsongs
that will have gone extinct before he
learns to tune his own ears up.

It Is Raining Again

for Lucy Blu

The soft rain, the bare ticks from clouds
too heavy to contain themselves anymore.
Sometimes in New Orleans it is hard to tell
the difference between a cry of joy, a cleansing cry
and someone who just came here to give up
as they gasp out grief in an alleyway or in a bar.
Laughter is close behind the pain here. Or ahead of it.

Anyway, rain is ticking onto statues of generals
statues of musicians, onto pigeons whose orange
claws brighten. Silver chains of rain slink
into the sewer or pool in low spots on asphalt.
Trickles dive off rooftops down long links
of copper gutters, spill onto the sidewalk

as lovers stroll past. Rain sidles down
where the many-colored pigeons
bathe in a shimmer of puddle.
As pairs head back to hotel rooms
of urgency and joy, an older couple
sits under an awning. Their love
exactly as it is here, intact
while they sip, pass a warm cup slowly
back and forth, hand often touching hand.

Wasted Nights

Emptiness and lust drove me into the thrum.
I'd watch women's wrists cock
fingers coil around their drinks. We'd get
doubled in bar-back mirror glass
the way verbiage and intention double.

All that was pent up reeled us out
onto blues-band, barroom floors. Coughed us
back into star-mingled, street-wet
ravenous minutes by the car side. Stuff
that goes bump, that goes bump.

Later, together, came a ghosting of what I am.
I'd go light as smoke. Then the roll, the drift
within that sea of sleep, that one long
swallow of the hereafter beside
a warm heave of flesh.

If I got up first, if she wanted to let
bones stew within a deeper inertia
I'd pause to savor how her hair
spread across the pillow, storm-tossed.

I'd hit the pavement where the strength
of the sun came on me sharp
as a chef's blade slivering up
thin rounds of the radish that was
my earth-cooled, dirt-born heart.

Greek Coffee

Have you ever wanted to strangle a friend
no matter how hard he would thrash and push?

Nick and I had been up past moon-set to whoop
and stomp from camp fire to camp fire in New South
Goat-sack Mississippi at an annual bash held
under the sparks of Orion's belt by a potter
who threw delicate Raku pieces cradled in straw.

He invited the entire Art and Classics departments
along with reprobates, half-bakes, and stray debutantes
out of the city to camp, imbibe, hoot, dance
as if there was no end to it while hills rolled
off in every direction, darkly secret with
Mississippi's grim resolve. Disturbed
from their rounds, coyotes glared, lit irises
reflected at the edge of the woods.

That night some bearded satyr grabbed my lapels
and shouted into my face, "I see you at every
weird party I go to." At which I blinked, smiled.
Beyond provocation I shook my head and sauntered off.
Found a twisty little grad-student's-wife to get to know

in the biblical way in the cab of Nick's Silverado.
Eventually some forty of us bivouacked on dells and knolls.
Woke to dew. My Greek friend Nick had a little blaze going
rubbed his hands to warm them as kettle water came to a boil.
Nick had a metal cup and a spoon with a ceramic design
in its bowl. Nick stirred his coffee till it went from thin to thick
from thick to granular. Nick stirred and stirred.

A crow at the forest's edge cawed as the spoon
scrapped along cup metal. Nick hunched. The crow cawed.
There is only so much that a hung-over man
by a campfire in Mississippi can be asked to endure.

The Dancers

It is two in the afternoon. Two, on this rag-tag
stretch of beach in Cajun paradise, Grand Isle.
At the point where surf churns up, pelicans
pump and glide inches above bronze sea caps.

We are four. Languishing. Dangled across soccer chairs. Swizzled.
We sip, gab, gossip, reminisce in the total glut of Saturday.
The full blare of a March sun bakes bones. I squint.
Nudge feet into sand as my skin drinks strong wind on this

sand-strip, barrier island. This extreme border of America
during extreme times but under the least extreme of conditions.
There is only one couple. They are old enough to have
picked up crow's feet. Old enough that they should have children

darting in and out of waves, burying themselves up to the neck
in sand. Instead, they are here alone, drunk-ass-drunk by two.
Their hips swirl as surf crashes but they are oblivious
gloriously immured, melded, eyes locked onto one another.

An hour ago, they left chairs, a shade cover. He has a boom box
hoisted up on his shoulder. His arm, muscled by years of labor
effortlessly lifts to curl up around the radio whose blast is
thankfully blanketed by gulf winds so that we cannot make out

whether the strains of song are country thrum or the cheap fire
of rock and roll, though they are only sixty feet away.
Feet churn, hips roll, loll, dip. Slow and mesmerizing swell
of two bodies immersed together into a sweet, drunken stir

of a Saturday's roux upon deeply brown sands, in the close
heat of a March sun, unblocked. Cooked until they cannot
tell where surf or sun stop and where their selves begin.
It is Saturday, effortless Saturday. It is two, only two.

Folding Church Chair

I rented a shack shielded from an asphalt lane by a row
of Ligustrum and at the back, 60 feet off a rail line.
It had running water but no electricity. 25 dollars a month.
The windows were blown out. Immediately, I bleached
the outhouse, made shutters from tomato stakes and plywood.
Under water oaks, the roof line bent like a harmonica note.

I still have a chair that was the first piece of furniture
I put into that house. I picked the chair up one afternoon
as I glided my bicycle down 11th street
and spied a door cracked open that led
into the basement of an abandoned church.

As my eyes adjusted to the dark, I made out
overstuffed furniture, a makeshift bar, tables
with folding legs, cards and dice. No whiskey.
Empties from those who'd taken over
the church basement. Mostly there were
fold-up, metal chairs. I lifted one, carried it
on my bike to my rent shack by the tracks.

For a while that brush-painted, maroon chair
was the only furniture I had other then
a rude, pine table the former resident
had left behind and a loft bed
I made to save space. I spent time
in the company of crickets on a porch
where it was easy to play a flute.

That chair sits on my patio now, reminds me
that I have the hands of a thief, that I have known
a time when poverty and privation were
as good as any current degree of ease or comfort.

It stays because come sunset
I like to plop down, take in every lilt
and note of what songs whistle
tick and hum from dusk shrubs.

Summer Shivers

My oldest was twelve the summer
I saw the ad for an above-ground pool
14' in diameter, sand filter, 42" high.
I'd get home from appointments
that stretched toward dusk with enough
light left to go into the backyard.
Bend and shovel as our stately Mastiff posed
in long and doubled shade. Windless evenings
where you sweat standing, I topped grass
under a tall chinaberry, leveled surface dirt.
Then puzzled out and fit a jumble
of metal tubes on which blue plastic hung.

Although the girls would come out to get tossed around
split sides laughing for the splash, I think they were
a little embarrassed by this chintzy, above-ground pool
the way the bourgeois always are of proletariat relatives.
They preferred videos, quiet games, talk.
Maybe three friends got in twice the whole summer.
It was me pulling weekends and doubles, who'd
slip in after dark, after the children went to bed
while my wife pretended to be absorbed
in yet another docu-drama. Those nights
barn owls' drawn calls were the only other
entrance into cool on the landscape.

Weeks on end when pavement scalded bare feet
I'd sink down with a beer in hand. Wait till
city-sky blanked enough to let stars show. Sip.
Almost ritual, that immersion, that divesting
oneself of the day. The rising shrill of crickets
whoosh from nearly traffic were nothing beside
the waiting for and the arrival of emptiness.
Sock back beer. Crawl out to the hammock.
Swing enough so wind could rake across my chest.
Shiver. Shiver under star spikes. Under dark branches, shiver.

I'm a Magpie on Dauphine St.

Magnolia blooms are big as plates clattered into piles
atop steaming hot steel counters in the backrooms
of restaurants in old New Orleans. Ramshackle platters
of blooms with fabulous, decadent stamen, powdery
and over-pollinated as a streetwalker's mascara.

And New Orleans is the best place to eat or fuck anywhere at all
in this whole slopped-out gumbo of an era. Except that
in the instant that anyone eats or comes, no one could care less
where they are because we get so completely launched
into diamond-pure being that everything else disappears.
Then comes back and that's why you want to be in New Orleans.
There's probably sticky stuff still glazing that restaurant plate
from bananas foster. Stars, streetlights intermingle, buzz, swarm.

Magnolia leaves are crisp as playing cards and the deep green
a miner would find wiping a fresh vein of jade to life
with a dripping bandana, eyes growing luminous with greed
in cave quiet. The leaves fold shade in upon each other
stay cool as parchment throughout blazing summers.

Though nothing can grow under magnolia, shade
gets thick enough to draw drafts. A sort of whispering
sanctuary pulls in sodden bums that lay out newspapers
sprawl, or prop against the trunk. Cats sleep. Hounds hunker.
Toddlers come, pluck up a bud or gum wrapper, haul it back
to offer up as gifts at the altar of their parent's attention.

Under the branches small girls with voices set
in the minor keys of loneliness, lift toy cups
off toy saucers, nurse a doll they've either drug
across dirt or carried in bent arms with a dedication to love.

The woman coming toward me now on Royal St.
has cheek, neck and arm skin that has tiny, little beads
within it, is almost atomized-soft the way a magnolia bloom
radiates what springs up immaculate on this earth.

Raw

I am most comfortable
gobbling oysters off the half-shell
in mid-February, a month
with two Rs captured
between the F from Freeze
and a "y" whose loop whips off
towards March and redemption.

A month where bitter gusts
can sweep leaves in behind you
at the door to swirl about the room
mad as a witch hat on a witch
possessed by a new mischief.

On a bed of diamonds
a dozen oysters shiver, iced
but still exuding a must
from their previous bed of rank muck
reed roots and marsh water.

The waft of procreation and creation
still on them as they dazzle
our buds for an instant
while the slithery glob
overwhelms the mouth
like a lover's tongue plunged deep.
Then it jiggles down the throat
leads us toward March and redemption.

My Drug of Choice

for William Hathaway

When Li Po dropped down
out of the stars on a frayed rope
he had me listen to how taut
the cricket's voice gets from all
its gnawing on dried leaves.
"Landscapes, creatures shape
each other," he said. Then we
knocked some back until the moon
quietly hobbled off to a bed of pine.
In the morning Li Po disappeared into
a speck down a trumpet vine flower
that I'd thought was all orange until he
continued to shrink and make his
slow descent into a yellow so buttery
I worried he could suddenly slip
the length of that sheer flute.

In Belize I snorkeled through a coral forest.
Butterfish slipped sideways
through encrusted gaps.
Clownfish drifted, whisked, wobbled.
I looked through jellyfish and anemone
that glowed with pastel lights.
The veined fans of a purple coral
swayed with the tempo of waves.

After I got stateside, I told everyone,
"It's like dreaming while being awake."
and it was, except that now I do it
all the time and thank every poet
I've every read and any star that's
chanced its way into my vision.
More than that, I dream awake with this pen,
this vein I pour my longing through.

Danged If You Do

I bought one bucket of canna lily
maybe fifteen years ago. By root
by rhizome they spread and soon
started to bury beloved rose buds
under their vault and shade.

I dug the lilies up, hauled them to the back
where tall stalks could block out the neighbors.
Made a nice patch next to an old metal post
        where the lady that owned this property
        through the 60s, 70s, 80s once hung
        towels, blouses, linen out to dry.

I laid a ring of old Chicago bricks
        that I got from a heap
        at a construction site after I'd
        asked the contractor for the right
as a rim to set the garden off.
Now the lilies crowd out into the yard.
I'd have to hack them back
to find those ore-red bricks again.
A veritable riot of broad green blades
and stalks clatter in spring wind.

They still sneak back up by the roses.
So every year I shovel them up
spirit stalks away to a far corner.
Tough as roaches, these. Survivors.
If I leave a single shred no more
substantial than a clipped cuticle
anywhere at all, next spring

I get a fresh half-dozen stalks
nine inches off the old spot.
They imbibe rain. Crimson tongues
hiss at me in broad light.

Sunday Reading at the Maple Leaf

If I've got the time I like to hop
inside a mockingbird's song
as the creature jockeys its way
through a bright afternoon.

I'll slip it some gin, splash of sweet summer gin
as we tool around where bamboo is still cool
where sideways branches of the elderberry can lend
an excellent perch after huge drops of rain
have flung themselves down on the city that care flat forgot.

You cannot tell how close you are to the river
from the patio at the Maple Leaf Bar
until you hear tugboats blow low, blow long.
That's when you start to feel all the dreams
of our grandfathers, forgotten desires of grandmothers
making their way down from graveyards in Ohio
bone fields of Montana, pastures in Minnesota
from under tombstones in Louisville, from lonesome
Memphis sepulchers. Dreams leach through soil
make their way into this slow, brown river
nod south toward the Gulf of Oblivion.

If you've given that mockingbird
just one too many to tipple
after rains tumbled freely over
a landscaped ruled by its waterways
you can halfway expect
to stumble out onto the sidewalk
and hear a gondolier cry out
as he strokes a strong oar to round
the corner of Dante St., turn onto Oak.
So you clamber aboard.
You rock your way west into sunset.

Corner of Royal and Franklin, 8:20 AM

Pigeons at the Flora Café in New Orleans
drink their colors in from puddles
while a great naval battle
sounds throughout the sky.

Water from rain that stopped half an hour ago
gets lifted in skirts of mist
behind cabs and pickups.

Leaves on the moonflower vine
have the dark face of a silent film's paramour
who has turned away, turned away slowly
into the shadow of forever.

If you spill crumbs outside the Flora Café
you'll see a flock lift off phone lines
descend to strut, red talons on concrete.
Just before landing, dove's wings burst open
into a light-shot sphere.

Kitty-corner, in front of Big Daddy's Bar
a band of men and women
who have survived the night
gab, laugh, shift weight
apropos of exhaustion, apropos
of lust, apropos of escape.

One more sip of java and my arteries
will shoot up like so many stamen
inside the flower of this indolent city.

CHAPTER IV

Meditations

There Wasn't Much of a Winter

This year ginger blooms blush
tissue-thin, launch in clusters
then burst open ore-red, saffron
long-tongued, almost obscene
on their green broad-leaf beds.

A month ago I was beside a glacial lake—
phantasmagoric azure and ice wavered
and meshed beneath a snow-cap.

That day Incan-sacred Salkantay shed rock
in a series of avalanches that we were told
would have been unheard of five years back.
Now the snow line slips up its hem.

Here the Mississippi is at record height
from floods in Iowa, Missouri, Kansas.
Tornadoes appear by the dozens
skirt across their midwest dance floor.

Though the throats of tree frogs
still open full and ululate for hours
through pointless spells of night

there are fewer birds every year
fewer nests. I am snug, content
loving my lovely flowers
as the world we've known
gets erased around me.

I Talk to a Dove

Tipped by a spare rain, leaves tremble
branches get swept. All is tin-pan
and smoked-glass. Begrudgingly cold
the way a wrung out cloth set by
the kitchen sink keeps cool a long while.
A hunched dove sits its bush.

What I want to know is why
it is important to say this.
Not to say this, to say anything.
How it gives a right relation
to tell how a thing is as if

there is a flame that leaps between
what is and what is within
as my tongue starts to trip
along the back of my teeth
and breath, fluted breath
plays out within wind.

Carolina

Silvery braids of creek water
swirl in under a tree root.
Buttery bib of a warbler on ash branch.
A flattened gum wrapper.

Limbs, twigs down, deteriorating.
At eye-level along the path
two trunks swollen with large burls.
A creek shoots left, fans
angles back. Reeds glow
in what light can slant this low.

Splash of ferns behind. A fly
lands. I flick it. Wind and lemon
rush through, rattle the high canopy.

Later we sit on our friend's porch.
Quiet talk. Patter between sips. She
has tea, he beer. Renee, white wine.
Scotch in my mitt. Trees tick in mist.

Not far off an ambulance winds
up a mountain road and reminds me
that three years ago my mother traveled
dying then dead, under desperate sirens.
So, it comes clear to me
how effortlessly all this will go on
without any one of us.

Out Late in the Atchafalaya Basin

scores of egrets
pure as glass

their images
waver in shallows
between their legs

so much
champagne pink
they could be
looking through themselves
transformed into flamingoes

steadily sunset pivots
over cypress
into darkness

silence
swallows
what words
I had

black ink printed
on a page of night

West

fragile between
      tree branches
are those the   embers
of day
      extinguishing
or the tinder
      of lovemaking
igniting

I Cling to What I Can

Where have the silences gone?
I remember a limitless abandon of snow falling
to river ice. One set of skate lines, alone
on a gloved and coated hour in utter dark
all the others gone back to their families.

There is a congestion, a contagion, an
inflammation of sound. Gas pumps blast
video ads. At the mall faux stones
laid beside aster sound out the hit parade.
The interstate's whoosh fills forests.

I think of my block as dopey, calm despite
weed-eaters, lawnmowers, circle-saws, chain
saws, air-conditioners, water pumps. Staccato
of hammers that drive nails into shingles.

Last month I drove across Texas.
Hoisted on a backpack.
Marched up switchbacks.
Stone, rock, juniper, pine.
Plants that root in crags.
Drank from a canteen.
Slept shoulder against dirt.

I listened the way a hunter
sorts through twitches, shifts
in black on black beside black.
Heard stone be stone.
Wind deposited itself into valley.
A cricket turned on bark. Leaves
wagged, interrupted spears from stars.

At Big Bend National Park

I stand on the South Rim, watch a peregrine
drift along the cliff wall, tilt its wing, shoot
kite out over Mexico, over Texas. Effortless.
Mountain crests break into dawn. Stone waves
repeated, repeating, filled with haze. Dawn-lifted
dawn-dispersing fogs shift through valleys
steep and stew inside this soft aurora.

I stand atop a precipice that took nineteen hours
to reach. Hiked up switchback trails. Packed in
three gallons of water. Two thousand feet of rise
in just a few miles. Slept on hard ground
through the silence of stars to get to this hour, this
spot beyond any tomorrow or yesterday. I begin
to read Eliot's East Coker, then Burnt Norton
to fog, to a peregrine, to this stone sea.

I read loudly, The Quartet's stentorian affirmations
which these mountains already know. I pronounce
the spirit-charged ether that is Eliot to the fog.
I give the landscape wind-torn, breath-raised
words from a bank clerk who barely
had enough shoulder to hold a suit coat.

I read sentences that meld together time and eternity
the way a welder's torch sears and marries metal.
I am here at last, joyfully pronouncing to indifferent powers
what that London bank clerk said, "In my beginning is my end."

January

On a day when dawn dials in
at minus twenty-three in distant Milwaukee
I imagine how my dear friend Gary
has mushed his Honda across that snowscape
to get to a local hospital and to be lulled
into an anesthesia-induced sleep

so that a surgeon's blade can
slice out a section of esophagus
that lies anterior to the curve of his cervical spine
replace his esophagus with a matching
3-D tube printed just for him.

In Baton Rouge I wake to see
black branches sprung and slender
willowy at points and back lit by dawn
behind an oak trunk that tilts slightly backwards.

Still, a few grace notes of leaves hang.
A norther drags through those branches
animates a slow, star-spare harp music
usually lost to me within the greater symphony.

Bounty and Thanks

I am baking pecans, fallen, filched
off dirt from beside ants and worms
while the sun speared branches, while mist
stewed late past dawn, while rain splintered
into yarrow and the clay dove cooed its clay coo.
You can taste the rich solitude of these nuts
slow-cured in hard and bitter shells.

I am baking them at 350 within a dark slosh
of molasses, egg, butter, sugar, vanilla, set down
into crusts I pulled from a freezer at the supermarket
checked out and slotted into our own Frigidaire.
Left the crust forgotten until now when it sends
a heated bloom belling out through every room.

Fills me with anticipation for tomorrow when
among family, I will savor a slice toward the end
of the day when we are all punchy and blotto and ready
to totter off to our individual cars, down our chosen highways
glide under tree branches that darken toward winter
swollen and numb with a mammalian blood murmur
of content. Given up, each in our separate conveyances
to a noiseless, almost inert, psalm of deep gratitude.

CHAPTER V

On Becoming

Yes, It Was an End

The tides were stealing the light of morning
and my children from me. Stealing the light in their hair
when they woke to drag a doll or teddy down the hall
because they needed cereal and they needed it
right away in the house I was not ever
going back to with a wife whose eyes
were already distant and drowned in the sea.

I picked my way toward seals' arched backs and yelps.
The shoreline flared and shattered
as waves broke, absorbed into sand
then crashed against its edge.

To my right, haphazard piles, a rocky jigsaw
where aquamarine and copper ingots flashed
and indulged themselves in dazzling arrays
flared for transitory instants but held a minute longer
in stone's seal-slick pockets and crannies.

Little was holding as the tide slipped off
carried away crabs, kelp strewn across
degraded planks and pulled
at the two legs of hope I had left.

The sea was everywhere, dazzling beside seals
as it took away what it could, lick by lick.
There was so much sacred need under the tilt
of a seagull's wings that wind could never fill it.
Wind could not take loneliness from any beak
or mouth along a shore where loneliness lives
in the wind and loss repeats itself in wave's crash.

Among stone, seals, and sand, gray can be
an eternal season and the sea steals one, by one, by one.
First it takes the coast, wraps it under blinding mist.
My children were taken from me where seals' yelps
get drowned and now the rise and blow
of a whale is the only heart I have left.

How to Heal

After my first marriage
I rented a quiet bungalow
on W. Sorrow Blvd.
Slept with windows open
near a cave formed
by live oak branches.

I might as well have been
a hundred miles beyond
the final post where Ma Bell
could stretch her copper wire lines
out into reckless wilderness.

It was a time for me
and what breezes turn pages
of a book left open on grass
to spend hours together, chum up.

Light and shadow furred on tabletops
furred up and down the baseboards.
I was living not in the world but under it—
the sort of hermit mole you meet
halfway through a children's book.

Days went on into infinity
with the terrible sameness
a spoon comes to know
in its spoon drawer.

For a year everything came in spoonfuls—
dawn, tragedy, new women,
cereal. All of it on W. Sorrow Blvd.

at an address anyone visited
only while I was out
and no one was let into
while I was there.

I Had Fallen

variation on a theme by Lawrence Durrell

I was with the one who tainted everything
in early March on a slope between
two camellias by the city-park lakes.
Her head and shoulders rocked back
into crimson blooms that had dropped
into soil. More flowers exploded
off the ends of camelia branches.

We had driven away from a party
to ferry a friend home. After
I let him out, rounded the corner
my fingers started ripping a hole
in her fishnet, working their way
to her moan. A little after we came
she said, "I hope your wife knows
how lucky she is to have you."

I had fallen off into moonlight.
Searched the sky. Tried to align
star clusters into a jagged design
to imagine an ancient, hidden constellation.
Image of the broke-neck body
of some obscure, Paleolithic deity
who wrenched sinews in knots
as he first formed the human heart.
Star-crusted outline of him hanged.

All That Then

I never should have let you go.
Though you were already married
I never should have let you go.

Though he came to my house
in his Ford with a gun in his pocket
seemed then just one more flea
on earth's hide—a miserable
anarchist made of anguish
and confusion who brandished
his pistola at me as if that had
any chance of being a solution

and handed me the letter you wrote
as he stood over you or stormed
from room to room in the upstairs flat
whose windows filled with mimosa
and crepe myrtle that summer.

Flat that was all the two of you
could afford back then. Flat up
an enclosed stairwell where my
footsteps never sounded again.

I don't know where you are.
I have moved on. I have not
moved on. I have never known
another woman who could
have so much rain falling
through her eyes at once.

I Gave It Up

Back when I played golf regularly
it was half a round at most
usually toward sunset when the links were empty.
While other men parked their cars
back under car ports the sun hauled itself west
and weakened enough for dirt and vegetation to relax
exhale a steamy osmosis up over the greens.

My drives would disappear in their trajectories
while daylight tilted into strawberry, tangerine
apple-green. I had to track the ball down in tiny
grass nests. Having finished the finale appointments
of my chock-full days, the one thing I wanted was

not to go home yet. Not to face the bitter face
bickering tongue, unmatchable expectations
of a soured marriage. Though really as soon as
I hit the door, I shed my business clothes. Slipped
on gym shorts. Led my girls out into the haunts
of our neighborhood. Ambled exhausted for
minutes with their voices close besides, while
crickets began to sound in another too-short night.

I never did get any good at golf. Only good
at leaving her. But then, that is one of the best things
that ever happened to me and probably to my children.
Our corrosive angers eventually dissipated
in the stew of hours, loss and hope.
Still, I like to be alone at sunset and just after
while the earth gets heavier and heavier
and the sun disappears from our separate trajectories.

Why I Don't Drink Tequila

The last time was on a Mardi Gras weekend
when friends blew in from Houston.
Took us downtown to a recording studio.
People crowded around a piano jamming out tunes
or wandered out the back door where the owner
had placed a ring of patio chairs—aluminum with
plaid webbing. Furniture you could lift with a finger.

So, after a few rounds when they turned the jam up
we raised those lounge chairs up over our heads
to do some sort of wacko conga line. Then set them
back onto concrete. Plopped our drunk asses down.
Some went off to the bathroom to do lines.

It was hot as I sat there staring at downtown brick.
The Tequila suggested that I could shinny
straight up one of the water pipes strapped to a brick wall—
like I had spider inside of me. My friend caught my ankle
when I was about eight feet up, pulled me back down.
He said, "What the hell are you doing?" I didn't know.

By this time, I'd already driven my wife home
to take care of the kids. I was ripped and things
weren't going too well for the two of us anyway.
So, I sat there with the music flowing, eyed a red-head
who was pouring out and serving up marguerites
freely as poker chips on a Vegas holiday.

I had a hum in my head. A real good hum
and she was knock-out. So, we struck it up
and found a chorus. We bent into each other.
I was guzzling her frothy Margaritas. She smelled
real good. Then some Boy Scout showed up

at our elbows as we kept dipping closer and closer
into each other's warmth and I eyed the guy
I thought she'd come with on the other side
of the room by the piano, singing.

So, the Boy Scout up and asked us real frank-like
"How long have the two of you been married?"
Which froze us both. Sent my mind scurrying
like a roach when you hit the wall switch.
I backed up, went home pretty soon after that.
Except that on the way I banged into a Nissan
at a red light. Swooped into our driveway
with a fender I'd had to pull back off the tire.

I gave me wife plain-lame explanations.
Which was alright because my wife
had given up on me long before that
and I'd already given up on her though
it would take four more years and massive
tectonic shifts of emotion to finally crack us apart.
Part of me has always wanted that red-head though
I've never seen her again. Till I do, I don't drink Tequila.

Somehow, January 2017

Well, mom, I have been hip to hip in
the same bed with one angel for a decade
since we hauled her two cats, twenty-seven
potted plants and a ten-foot Australian fern
over here. Had to slow drive that ten-foot fern
down back streets, cocked-up, wagging
wind-wrenched for four miles out the
open trunk of my black Mitsubishi.

She brought all of it—jewelry, photos
a red couch, dresses, a slew of shoes—on one
of those winter days where clouds go steel.
It was five months after Katrina
sent six hundred thousand Louisiana lives
into an entanglement of hell, left us
to sweat through brutal heat without electricity
but otherwise, unscathed.

I think you'd want to know that your youngest
the one that never could handle marriage
despite more attempts than most
has something other than a pillow to nestle at night
counts himself among the lucky, stays well nourished.
Doesn't get lonely yet can still sit solitary
in my backyard that you never got to visit
though it seems somehow you do.

The Obvious

I am looking for something that is
close by. I have spent a lot of my life
looking for things that I put down
a minute ago, before the faucet leaked
and I went to get pliers and a screwdriver
but all I could find were Phillips-heads
until I went to the tool chest in the closet.

Anyway, now I am looking for something
the way a geneticist does even as she sips a coke
after spending hours imaging patterned codes
on a computer screen hooked to a microscope.
Looking for parts that haven't yet been seen
or parts that have been overlooked. What
writes the codes in the first place.

The obvious. Something that tends to
avoid grey matter. Stays in the white, in
the blank undifferentiated flood of sunlight
that slowly turns blue as swirling motes abundantly
reflect light's abundance. I seem to know so much
these days about things that just pop up. Provinces
in Afghanistan, the way free electrons in carbon
can be bonded within plastics, the nakedness of
movie stars. Random crawl. I don't really

know a damn thing except that light
sweeps through the room every morning
as you make your way back to bed
from the bathroom in the hall.

Black Dutch

I stood, suited, sentry, in front
of two tall candelabra and your casket
as I waited for your family to file by.
I find you next to me in the bed
Motionless, brought back from the creamy
unrustled silk the undertaker fixed you in.
Here you lay, as you should, on your side.
Hips, knees buckled. Blanket tucked to your back.

Your father told your family you were all
"Black Dutch," which means part Indian.
Cherokee most likely. I could never
see it in your frame or features. Only
in the way a stillness envelopes you
when you sit or walk or sleep.

I remember coming in from outside
after you first moved in. I could
never find you. I would walk by
the room where you were, keep
wandering the house till I came back.
Got quiet enough myself to really see.

This morning you were next to me
as you have been for over a decade.
I lay stunned, exhausted by sleep
having been robbed of you in dream
and having recovered you in so short a time.

Softly I rested my hand on the blanket
over your ribs. Very softly.

The Weight

It is incumbent upon me just
to lie alone at the star point
where darkness begins
to turn the page of day.

Love and lust
twine through me.
Aside from this twining
of your absent skin
into the twisted fibers
of the dark and lust

there is only
the weight of dawn
that rests like a lover's hand
upon my chest.

Valentine

Tonight as the grackle
rests on a branch in the forest
as the grackle preens
his reflections of starlight
we will make love.

Dusk

Sunset's mink shawls
and blood-stained scarfs reflect
in the stem of my gimlet's crystal.

Under bushes, ink pools.
As a lavender cloud drifts east
I grow weightless as a child
with a child's quicksilver movements.

What has dispersed
are clouds of solitude
that piled inside my chest.
A tripled brood. One
my ailing sister. Two
my eldest brother's death.

Three, worry about Renee as she
moves through our evening kitchen
fridge to counter to stove.
Renee's eyes turn more murky
each year, as if the world
is trying to leave her.

Tonight frets lose their grip
as dark cumulus
dissipate to pull west
by mandate of a regal sun.

Again

for Renee

Just off the eaves of our house
summer grass is speckled with fallen
crepe myrtle petals whirled as pubic hair.
In-woven petals crenulated pink
rill in soft swells of champagne.

These flowers have given out under
the merciless scorch of July afternoons
drift light as spiders down to blades.
Ants trek by. Roly-poly
grub along in the dirt.

Since I come to you again
like this, lost and bewildered
arms full of tenderness.

Since you take me in again
the way that grass and death
take everything in without question.

My Sixty-Fifth Spring

There are doorways
                into night sky.
Even doorways down
                into the forest floor.
Caves with cool drafts
                drenchings of darkness.

The open mouth of a women
                open blouse.
An utter profusion
                of possibility.
Cellos come to us
                lay their necks in our hands.
If I go to sleep for a hundred years
                under the lip of a mushroom
I will still remember the smells of lichen and molds
                in the dew when I wake.

Now I understand that I have never
                wanted anything
but to turn this doorknob, open this door.
                To gain access to this rain
again and again. The light rain you take
                with you over lawns
onto rooftops, into trees
                onto skin.

The rain that falls on cypress
             where birds hop
from branch to branch, nip
             under their wings.
So much light spread through out
             the trembling, falling
silver rain of you.
             To have tender shoots
crop up from dirt
             lift within me.

About the Author

Ed Ruzicka is the author of two previous full-length books of poetry, *My Life in Cars* and *Engines of Belief*. His poems have appeared in *The Chicago Quarterly Review, The Atlanta Review, Rattle,* and *Canary* as well as many other literary journals and anthologies. Ed has been a finalist for the Dana Award and the New Millennium Award. Currently Ed is spearheading a resurrection of the Poetry Society of Louisiana and stands to be deemed the reborn charter's first president soon after *Squalls* reaches stores. Ed was born in rural Illinois. He has two grown daughters, two small, well-loved grandchildren, two stepdaughters, and two step-grandchildren. Ed is an occupational therapist. He lives in Baton Rouge, Louisiana with his wife, Renee.

www.ingramcontent.com/pod-product-compliance
Lightning Source LLC
Chambersburg PA
CBHW022145160426
43197CB00009B/1436